Leonardo *and* Gabriel

Tim Tigner

Leonardo and Gabriel is dedicated to one of the two most influential men in my life, a man who passed before I published a single word, but whose actions travel through time to temper them all, my grandfather, the Reverend Doctor John Thompson Peters.

For more information on this novel or Tim Tigner's other thrillers, please visit timtigner.com

Introduction

Everyone knows the work of Leonardo da Vinci, luminary of the Renaissance. Ask a person to name a painting, and they will likely cite *The Mona Lisa*, even if they can't identify Leonardo as the artist. If pressed to name another artwork, they might well say *The Last Supper,* the mural that features in this book and is widely considered to be the most spellbinding narrative painting in history.

But Leonardo's contributions went well beyond those made with pigment and brush.

Da Vinci made breakthroughs in the fields of anatomy, aerospace, astronomy, dentistry, engineering, fluid dynamics, geology, the martial arts, mathematics, medicine, music and optics among others.

Many of those are represented by recognizable sketches, of which there are thousands. Perhaps most famous among them is the *Vitruvian Man,* which blends mathematics and art, and like the book you are about to read, endeavors to display the divine symmetry inherent in the universe.

Given the vast and diverse array of da Vinci's works, it is not hyperbole to say that the world has never known a greater mind. But brilliance is not synonymous with accomplishment. Intellect is but a tool. One cannot help marveling that Leonardo managed to accomplish so much in his lifetime. Nor can the ambitious help but hunger for his secret.

Scholars have concluded that three factors were fundamental to da Vinci's phenomenal output. One, his incredible intellect coupled with his insatiable curiosity. Two, his environment—Italy during the Renaissance. And three, his methodology.

This novella explores a possible fourth. A secret source of motivation. But let's not put the cart before the horse.

Regarding Da Vinci's methodology, it is worth noting that Leonardo relied on his own experiments and observations, rather than classroom learning, more than any other distinguished and prolific inventor. Referring to himself as "an unlettered man," Leonardo combined his unsurpassed powers of observation with his passion for experimentation to teach himself directly from nature. He considered this approach superior to book learning.

Thank goodness he did.

By methodically verifying things with his own eyes, Leonardo avoided the false conclusions and incorrect assumptions that routinely handicapped others. Errors akin to assuming that *the Earth is the center of the universe*.

Because of his proven ability to solve problems by beginning with a blank slate, Leonardo is the perfect hero for our story. If you wish to make the most of this intellectual adventure, I suggest that you attempt to mimic his open-minded approach. It won't be easy—if it were, there would be more Leonardos—but nothing ventured, nothing gained.

One final note. While the dialogue in this story is fictitious, the key artwork, people, relationships and many of the events are real. Leonardo did work for Duke Sforza, fight with the Prior of the church housing *The Last Supper*, and maintain a friendship with Niccolò Machiavelli, author of *The Prince*. Leonardo constantly fell behind schedule and ultimately failed to complete many of his most promising works. Fortunately, *The Last Supper* was not among those.

Enough background. Enjoy the story. I believe it will give you something to think about. It might even change your life.

— *Tim Tigner*

Torment

Leonardo Da Vinci was living a lie. It tormented him day and night.

For the first forty-six years of his life, he had chosen to ignore the war raging in his head. Alas, the ostrich approach was no longer an option.

Not now.

Not with the battle but inches from his face.

He set a paintbrush upon the scaffolding

and cracked his knuckles, one after the other. He'd been holding his favored brush for hours—without making a single stroke. Such introspective stints should not be problematic, but they were.

Although the sessions spent in contemplation were often Leonardo's most productive, generating the insights that elevated his artwork, the Prior presiding over his project was not convinced. In Gioffre's monastic world, idle hands were the devil's workshop.

Truth be told, on this particular occasion Prior Gioffre had a point. Leonardo had made no progress today. Despite giving the problem his full focus, he remained stumped and indecisive.

"You've been summoned by the duke."

The words shattered da Vinci's concentration like a rock through a window. After his senses regained their balance, Leonardo saw that Francesco had joined him on the scaffolding. "What does Sforza want?"

Leonardo's assistant gave a slight shrug. "Do you think he'd tell me?"

Of course he wouldn't.

The Duke of Milan, Ludovico Sforza, employed tens of thousands of men. He was a man of great power, pride, and prestige. He would not deign to confide in underlings.

Nor would he react kindly to being kept waiting. The man who paid the bills rarely did.

Leonardo found the duke in the courtyard of the royal residence at Castle Sforza. This was a welcome stroke of luck. Leonardo had designed the playful fountains that were its focal point. Delighting visitors young and old, the waterworks were a source of pride for Ludovico—and a constant reminder of Leonardo's genius.

Had the weather not been so temperate, they might be meeting in the Sala delle Asse. That venue would have been considerably less propitious, for Leonardo was well behind schedule in painting its ceiling. The challenge he faced with Sforza's fresco was entirely different from that of his current endeavor. The vegetable motifs the duke had requested were boring, and boring always ranked last on Leonardo's want-to-do list.

While he waited for his turn before the big chair, Leonardo's thoughts returned to the tormenting task he'd just abandoned. For three years, he had been faithfully planning and painting the climactic scene from the four gospels. *The Last Supper*. He was capturing the moment just after Jesus revealed that one of the twelve disciples at the table would betray him.

The enormous mural that covered an entire wall of the dining room was *almost* finished.

Only two small sections remained untouched.

Alas, they were the most important. The focal points that everyone entering the room was sure to study. The centers of energy and emotion. The faces of Judas and Jesus.

The latter was the source of Leonardo's torment.

Not the artistry involved in painting the son of God, but the hypocrisy.

Try as he might, Leonardo could not convince himself to truly believe in the God of the Bible. He couldn't reconcile the picture preached in Scripture with the suffering he saw. Therefore, he couldn't imbue his artwork with the authenticity it deserved.

How could the Almighty possibly permit the innocent to endure so much misery? Leonardo knew no benevolent father who would allow his children to suffer.

Leonardo's faith also snagged on the *children* part. Scripture says *God so loved the world, that he gave his only begotten Son.* But weren't we all supposed to be His children?

As Leonardo stared at the space that should already contain the holy face, he again attempted to find a way forward. There were only three options. One, *ignore the problem.* This was the alternative he absolutely dreaded, for it would make his masterpiece imperfect. Two, *embrace faith.* The irony of that solution was not lost on Leonardo. To embrace faith, he would need to forsake his greatest God-given ability. His reason. Or three, *reconcile faith with reason.* This was by far his favored approach, but he did not hold out hope. The great philosophers had all failed to square that circle.

Nonetheless, Leonardo found his torment exacerbated by the constant feeling that he was close to finding that philosophical path. On the verge of grasping something that Aristotle, Augustine and Aquinas had all missed. A grand unifying insight that could reconcile faith with reason. Some—

"Leonardo!"

Da Vinci looked up to see Duke Sforza standing before him. His Grace was garbed in a rose-colored cloak resembling Leonardo's own, but stitched with silver and buttoned with gold.

Despite their similar age and dress, Sforza projected a presence entirely different from Leonardo's. He presented an air of power accented by a hint of danger. This was an image his voice reinforced. "It's a double-edged sword, that mighty intellect of yours. I sense that it rarely allows you a peaceful respite."

"You wanted to see me, Your Grace?"

"Yes, and I suspect that you know why.

Prior Gioffre called on me earlier. He's not a happy monk. He has arranged for King Charles VIII to take mass at Santa Maria delle Grazie during his visit to Milan this weekend. Needless to say, such an honor would pay dividends for a generation to come. But Gioffre insists you have put the privilege in jeopardy by failing to finish the very mural that has attracted His Majesty."

Leonardo began to speak, but Sforza held up a hand.

"Gioffre also tells me that yesterday you spent twelve hours staring at the painting without so much as lifting your brush. He said that's not the first time you have indulged in idleness. He added that you have also been spending an inordinate amount of time in the ghetto entertaining drunkards while your work goes unfinished. Is that true?"

Leonardo had lifted his brush, but knew better than to quibble over semantics. "In essence, it is true. But in both instances, I was working. Smearing pigment is the easy part, My Lord. Knowing precisely what to paint is the challenge."

"And for this you are gaining guidance from the ghetto? I fail to find the connection."

"Where better to behold the face of a Judas than among the thieves and criminals?" Leonardo asked.

Sforza shook his head. "And Jesus. Are you seeking Him in the slums?"

Leonardo was not about to reveal the true source of that dilemma. "Inspiration comes from strange places, My Lord."

"I won't presume to argue with you regarding inspiration. I don't want to argue with you at all. Promise me this, Leonardo. Promise me you will complete *The Last Supper* by week's end. Promise me that I, as the painting's sponsor, will not have to apologize to the King."

Leonardo took a deep breath. "I promise."

"Good. You better get back to it then."

"Yes, My Lord."

"But first, tell me one thing. When do you intend to finish my ceiling?"

The Last Supper

Leonardo Da Vinci. 1490s

Zoom on Judas (left) and Jesus (right)

Gabriel

Leonardo raced from Castle Sforza to the convent of Santa Maria delle Grazie. After leaving his panting horse with a stout stable boy, he walked straight to his scaffolding. He climbed the creaky wooden structure to a well-worn plank poised twenty-five feet above the floor and settled in before the spot where two faces should be staring back at him.

Again he picked up his paintbrush.

Again nothing happened.

Apparently, inspiration did not strike simply because a duke commanded it.

Leonardo's lack of progress did not prevent onlookers from assembling below. Dozens stopped by on most days to watch him work as though painting a mural were a theatrical attraction.

Leonardo ignored them, as he always did.

One good thing about working in a church was that visitors were required to remain respectful. While their presence often produced a positive effect—the stimulation of sitting high above an attentive crowd— today the audience only furthered the frustration of his indecision.

Leonardo found himself tempted to turn around and ask the observers what the face of God's only son should look like. Fortunately his tongue thought twice. The question would cause an uproarious scandal with an undoubtedly bitter end. So Leonardo remained seated with his back to the crowd, seeking internal inspiration.

Many hours into his meditation, he must have drifted off, for the next thing he knew, Leonardo found himself face to face with an angel. Or an *arch*angel, to be more precise.

Gabriel did not descend from a cloud or fly forth from shimmering light. He simply appeared there before Leonardo, the way figures in dreams always do.

Leonardo instantly recognized his heavenly visitor. Da Vinci had spent hundreds of hours contemplating, creating and perfecting Gabriel's every feature while painting *The Annunciation*. The archangel appeared exactly as the artist had rendered him—with curly locks, feathery wings, and a golden halo.

To Leonardo, the match made perfect sense.

It was his dream.

The archangel's voice, however, surprised him. Gabriel sounded like Andrea del Verrocchio, the true-eyed artist to whom Leonardo had been apprenticed in his youth.

"Greetings, Leonardo. I've come to give you a great gift."

Now there was an opening line you couldn't hear too often. Could that gift possibly be the obvious? Leonardo dared not hope. But then, why else would God send His messenger? "The solution to my struggle? You've come to give me faith?"

Gabriel smiled, bringing his angelic eyes alight like lapis on fire. "Faith will follow surely as day after night. But what I'll be giving you is a much greater gift."

A greater gift than faith? Considering the source, that was a profound promise. Leonardo could not guess where this ethereal encounter was going—but he found himself very eager to get there.

Being an angel rather than a demon, Gabriel did not keep him waiting. "I'm going to give you the ability to render God. First in your mind, then on the mural. I'm going to help you know Him, wholly and completely."

Leonardo found himself unable to respond. His mind swirled with the color of hope and the light of excitement. His skin began to tingle so severely that he feared he would wake. There was nothing he loved more than the moment of discovery, and this, if accurate, would be the greatest revelation of all.

Since Adam first walked the Garden of Eden, no man had truly and completely understood God.

Although many claimed to.

Most were men whose power, position or

prestige depended on that special status. Leonardo had pressed more than a few in an attempt to end his torment. He'd cornered priests in confessionals and bishops in bars. All had evaded specifics with talk of *mysterious ways.*

But this is just a dream! Leonardo's excitement dwindled as reality intruded. Dreams had a penchant for being too good to be true. *Yes, that had to be it. It would be silly to presume otherwise. Surely the real Archangel Gabriel would not bestow such a unique and precious gift upon a nonbeliever.*

But Gabriel's image failed to fade as discovered dreams usually did. This emboldened Leonardo to ask his question. "Why give me this gift? Why not a monk or a priest? A cardinal or a king?"

The voice of Verrocchio did not hesitate. "I chose you because of your mind, Leonardo. No living monk or priest, cardinal or king, has an intellect your equal."

Leonardo could almost buy that. Ideas flowed from his mind like water from the Dolomites in spring. He had made scores of significant breakthroughs. Discoveries in art and medicine, optics and astronomy, science and engineering. But not religion.

Gabriel sensed his hesitation. "None of them has a mind *as pure* as yours."

The clarification did not help Leonardo. If anything, it boosted his bafflement. Of all the people on the church grounds at that moment, Saint Peter would likely count him among the most sinful. At least in regards to religious practice. "I don't understand."

"It's not a matter of piety, but rather one of perspective."

"Perspective?"

Gabriel clarified. "People naturally look upon God from a selfish point of view. Humans cannot help it. They do not pursue the unseen for altruistic reasons. They seek it in an effort to improve their lives. This leads mortals to make mistakes by interpreting the unknowable in advantageous ways.

"When it comes to religious matters, this self-serving reflex is especially robust among the monks and priests and cardinals and kings. They shape their lives and draw their benefits in accord with favorable definitions and interpretations. Therefore, it is beyond them to consider the Almighty with an unbiased mind."

Leonardo immediately conceded the point. Everyone attempted to interpret issues and events from a favorable perspective. Most sought their own greater glory. People took credit for their successes and blamed others for their failures. It was preprogrammed. Ordained. Human nature.

Gabriel pressed on. "This individual bias extends to institutions. Every church and chapel, every sect and denomination, derives power from its position as a gateway to God. And like all businesses, each prefers a monopoly. Exclusivity on the ultimate real estate. Ownership of the eternal soul.

"Therefore, all religions tout themselves as *the one true path*. All emphatically reject and renounce any insight or interpretation that would allow men to bypass their particular collection plate in the quest to know God."

Leonardo appreciated the argument, but

then of course he would. As a figment of Leonardo's imagination, Gabriel was working with inside information. Nonetheless, his thoughts snagged on a prickly point. Religions were made up of more than the men that ruled them. "What about sacred texts like the *Bible* and the *Quran*?"

Gabriel raised a slim finger. "Where do you think those sacred texts came from?"

Leonardo had not previously considered that question.

Gabriel knowingly continued without pause. "Neither they nor any other earthly document was penned by God or delivered by angels. All were composed by men, for men. *The Last Supper* you are painting, for example, is described in each of the four gospels. The gospels according to Matthew, Mark, Luke and John. Four *men*. The provenance of those texts is right there in the titles.

"Don't get me wrong, the Bible and the Quran are full of wisdom and insight, but they are designed to be self-serving. Each was written to facilitate the growth of its religion. And, I should point out, no holy book accomplishes our goal. If any text truly imparted a clear and complete understanding of God, everyone would know it—and we would not be having this conversation."

"A fair point. But why doesn't Scripture include the revelation you promise to share?"

Gabriel grew a mischievous smile. "Surely you can deduce that answer from what we've already discussed." The phrase was a favored refrain of his favorite teacher, delivered one last time in Verrocchio's voice.

The challenge itself took Leonardo but a few seconds to solve. As soon as he did, he felt foolish for not having arrived at the conclusion unbidden. "The revelation doesn't serve the interests of the church."

"Correct. In fact, understanding how God works doesn't serve *any* organization's interests—and that creates serious problems. Kings and their counterparts constantly claim that *God is on their side*. It's a common tactic used to motivate and manipulate the masses. Anyone attempting to take that tool away would soon find his head bidding farewell to his neck."

Leonardo could only concur, sad and cynical though it seemed. "Coming back to my original question, I cannot help noting that there are many other intelligent men with what you call a pure mind. Notaries and philosophers, bankers and poets for example."

Gabriel nodded acknowledgment. "While that is true, virtually all your distinguished contemporaries know what they know from book learning. They swallowed what they were fed without filter or forethought. You, by sharp exception and stunning contrast, have made breakthrough after breakthrough by starting with a blank slate and building up your own beliefs with direct experiment and observation.

"Ironic though it may be, the fact that you are not a lettered man will assist you in this intellectual undertaking."

Leonardo's chest warmed as if lit from

within. His whole life he had suffered snobbish slights from his formally educated peers, men like Michelangelo and the Medicis. Wouldn't it be delightful if that perceived weakness proved to be his greatest strength? "I see."

Gabriel did not stop there. "Your trademark approach, no unproven assumptions, is the one we must take to properly paint an intimate understanding of God in your mind."

"Very well," Leonardo said. Ironically, he was too overwhelmed to think of a more erudite reply.

Rather than get right to it, Gabriel delivered a second shock. "I should confess at this point to having my own selfish motivations. This gift of understanding will help you become more productive. Given your great talents, that means the whole of humanity will ultimately benefit."

Leonardo did not know how to respond to flattery that predictive and profound. Fortunately he didn't have to.

"Are you ready to begin?" Gabriel asked

with a twinkle in his eyes.

Da Vinci was so eager to embark on the visionary voyage that his pulse quickened and his palms quivered—and his eyes opened.

Annunciation

Leonardo Da Vinci. 1470s

Niccolò

Leonardo awoke to a profound sense of excitement. His mind struggled for a second to identify the source, but as he sat up on the scaffolding the dream burst back to life. The visit. The discussion. The promise.

He looked around to ensure he wasn't still dreaming. The spectators had departed and the dining hall was dark, aside from the last light of a few flickering candles. How long had he slept? Apparently, for hours.

Leonardo pushed the common question aside in favor of reflecting while the revelations were fresh. Unlike the remnants of most dreams, he found that the images remained vivid and the dialogue crisp. He replayed the whole encounter, hoping to hammer it into long-term memory.

Once he was satisfied that the imprint was effectively embedded, Leonardo slid down the scaffolding. Again he was leaving *The Last Supper* behind—without brushing a single stroke.

Imprudent though that might be, he was too excited to worry about Prior Gioffre or even Duke Sforza at that moment. He had to discuss the dream. He needed to probe its intricacies and implications with another enlightened mind.

Leonardo knew the perfect person—if only he could find him.

Italy was the intellectual hub of the universe in 1498, and Milan was a major spoke. Although this meant there was no shortage of bright minds with whom to hold philosophical discussions, one particular foil struck Leonardo as certain to be both fruitful and safe.

The latter being no small point.

When visiting central city squares, it was

not uncommon to find heretics being burned at the stake. Poor souls who had offended the church. Nobody was beyond reach.

Years earlier, Leonardo had suffered two close calls himself after allegations of activities that ran afoul of church doctrine. Harmless trysts—with the wrong fellow. Fortunately, each accusation had been made anonymously, and therefore both were eventually dismissed—but not before Leonardo sweated his way through many a sleepless night.

With that experience front of mind, Leonardo pushed open the heavy oak door of Bella's Blackbird Tavern. A favorite of many courtiers, *the Blackbird* was located just inside the main gate of Sforza Castle. Whereas evenings there could get rather rambunctious with both celebrations and laments, breakfasts were typically sober affairs attended by people preparing for diplomatic battle.

Leonardo made his way to the corner table, a location providing a view of the entire establishment.

An irritated waiter with gnarled knuckles raised a ruddy palm. "That table is reserved."

"I'm meeting Niccolò."

Leonardo watched with satisfaction as the landscape changed. The eyes relaxed, then the muscles of the man's neck and shoulders. The words that followed were superfluous. "Aah, very well, sir."

"Raphael, don't you recognize Leonardo from Vinci?" Bella called from behind the bar.

"Oh," the waiter said, his eyebrows creating wrinkles as they rose. "Apologies, sir."

Leonardo nodded. "How soon do you expect Signor Machiavelli?"

Raphael walked to a window from which he could see the clock on Castle Sforza's central tower, one of the world's first public mechanical timepieces. "Any minute now."

As if purposefully proving the prediction, Niccolò entered The Blackbird two ticks later. His face darkened at the sight of the occupied table, but the cloud cleared when he recognized the intelligent eyes above the intruding beard. "The usual, for my distinguished friend and me," he announced to Raphael's obvious relief.

"Hello, Leonardo. This is an unexpected treat. To what do I owe the pleasure of your company at my morning meal?"

"I had a most unusual dream, one whose intricacies and implications reminded me of you. I thought we might discuss it."

Niccolò's eyelids creased. "I'm afraid I don't have much time today—early meeting—but I am interested in anything the great Leonardo has to say. What kind of dream?"

Niccolò wasn't the only one who knew which buttons to press. "A dream full of political, philosophical, and—" Leonardo leaned in to whisper, "religious intrigue."

Machiavelli responded with similar discretion. "So I'm to get a bit of heresy with my morning hash. Bring it on, my friend."

Raphael accented the request by delivering two plates of hashed turnips with egg and pork.

Leonardo continued to speak sotto voce,

describing his dream while they plowed through their plates. He began with the context of *The Last Supper* and left out nothing but the tormenting question that had undoubtedly instigated Gabriel's visit. He concluded by asking an open-ended question. "What do you think?"

With a side-set jaw and upward gaze, Niccolò set down his fork and raised a finger. "I should begin by saying that I have often dreamt the answers to my most vexing problems. There's something about unfettering the mind from the senses that is particularly conducive to breakthroughs." He raised his eyebrows, then added, "It usually happens when I've been struggling with something during the waking hours."

Leonardo took the bait without springing the trap. "The time has come for me to paint the face of Jesus in *The Last Supper*."

"That explains it," Niccolò said with a satisfied nod. "I must say, I find his logic fascinating. Gabriel's reason for selecting you, I mean."

"I thought you would."

Given the time constraint, Leonardo needed to move the discussion along, but considering the topic, he wanted to do so without a heavy hand. This was territory where the wise tread lightly, even among friends. "What do you make of Gabriel's analysis regarding the self-serving nature of man?"

"It's astute and accurate," Niccolò said without hesitation.

"Not overly skeptical?"

"Oh no. You could find an exception here or there if you looked hard enough, but at the center of any power structure, that observation applies nearly one hundred percent. Rising to leadership roles requires people to fall in line with the self-serving norms of their organization."

"Even when that organization is religious?"

"Absolutely. Self-preservation is an integral part of human nature—regardless of whether the power comes from a castle, a consortium, or a church."

Leonardo relaxed. "I worried I was being

too cynical."

"You're probably not being cynical enough. If you study the dynamics of power, you'll see that the skillful players and successful organizations don't just strive to maintain order within their ranks." Niccolò paused with raised fork while savoring his last bite of hash. "They also seek to manipulate the beliefs of *outsiders* in beneficial ways."

"You seem to have given this a lot of thought."

"I'm planning to write a treatise on the subject."

"Religious propaganda?"

"Heavens no. A political how-to manual. Advice princes can use to manipulate men and maintain power."

The two scholars sat in silence for several seconds, digesting their discussion along with their food. Only when he sensed that his companion was prepared did Leonardo pose the big question. "Do you think it's possible for a person to clearly comprehend God? To truly understand how He works?"

Niccolò turned toward Leonardo wearing a frank expression. Focused eyes, relaxed jaw, pressed lips. "I can only think of two possible reasons why humans couldn't. One, we're not sufficiently intelligent. If that is what has been holding us back, then you, my big-brained friend, may well be equipped to go where no one has gone before."

Niccolò raised a finger. "But I don't think that's it. At least, not according to what Gabriel told you. Your winged visitor didn't emphasize your incredible intellect. Instead, he focused on your tactics. Your method of discovery. That leads me to believe the second possible reason is more likely."

"And what reason is that?"

"If it's not *intelligence* holding us back, it must be *perspective*. It's quite possible that we've never looked at Him from quite the right angle. You have repeatedly demonstrated an unparalleled ability in that regard. Your weaponized chariot and colossal crossbow are excellent examples of the power inherent in a fresh point of view."

Leonardo ignored the compliments. "So

you think it's possible that I might actually come to know God before this is finished? Assuming Gabriel chooses to continue our conversation."

Niccolò strained to see the clock, then stood to leave. "I don't know about that, but I do know this: if the God you come to know is not the God of the Roman Catholic Church—you better not tell a soul."

Abilities

Leonardo felt better after *heresy over hash* with Niccolò, but he still struggled with scores of questions. His mind was swimming and he felt the urge to let his body do the same. He longed to visit his favorite bathhouse and splash about for a few hours. But alas, he could not risk the political pushback that would follow if he were sighted at yet another idle activity.

He briefly considered a quick dip in the Naviglio Grande's frigid waters, certain that even a few seconds would refresh his body and invigorate his mind, but the weather was just too menacing. So he snugged his cloak and rode his horse, Euclid, directly from the Blackbird back to Santa Maria delle Grazie.

Someone must have seen him coming, for he found Prior Gioffre standing before the scaffolding, waiting with crossed arms, an entrenched scowl, and squinty eyes that shone with satisfaction. *Hardly a pious pose.*

Leonardo had half a mind to turn around and take that swim after all. The idea of climbing to his perch like a monkey before his master was more than he was prepared to bear. Fortunately, inspiration struck before he corrected course. "It does my heart good, father, knowing that you will spend your day looking up to me."

While Gioffre's face flushed the color of Leonardo's cloak, the painter brushed past without a sidelong glance. Ascending the scaffolding, he resolved to put the prior out of his mind. Any additional attention would amount to giving the monk a victory.

After settling in before his unfinished work, Leonardo began to regret his decision to return. Convent dining halls did not inspire images of Judas. To find the face, expression and gestures that telegraphed the intent to betray God for money, he needed to walk among the sinners and scoundrels, the tricksters and grifters. He needed to go to the ghetto.

But not at midday.

The nefarious class emerged in the evening, when the wine was flowing and the low light concealing.

Regarding the painting's other glaring gap, the face of God, Leonardo pegged his hopes on Gabriel. But midday was not the time for that encounter either.

Or was it?

With a casual backward glance, Da Vinci confirmed that Gioffre had indeed moved on. Then he lay down for a nap.

Sleep came quickly, as it often did after excitement and stress.

So did his visitor.

"Thank goodness you're back," Leonardo said.

Gabriel gave him a learned look. "I never left. You just temporarily lost the ability to see."

Leonardo swallowed the surprising insight like a spoonful of honey. He'd never considered dreams in that context before. It was a simple but sweeping switch of perspective—one that opened up a whole new view of the world.

No doubt that was the intended effect.

No doubt that represented but a taste of the meal to come.

"Do you remember where we left off?" Gabriel asked.

"We were about to begin sketching God on a clean canvas."

"Exactly. We will start without assumptions and build upward from there." Gabriel glowed gold as he gestured from Earth toward Heaven. "For our first move, we will delineate the qualities that define God and only God. Each quality will, in effect, become a premise in our proof."

"Premises in our proof," Leonardo repeated. He was intimately familiar with the tactic of creating a case by logically linking postulates. Assembling and arranging supporting facts such that one could not deny the conclusion if he first accepted the antecedents and the logic that linked them.

"Let me make sure I've got this right," Leonardo said. "In essence, we will be solving for God?"

"Precisely. I like it," Gabriel replied with verve. "*Solving for God* summarizes it nicely."

This was bound to be interesting.

Gabriel raised an index finger. "Let us begin with the fundamental question, How is God defined?"

Leonardo hoped all the archangel's questions would be so easy. The answer was right there in the *Almighty* epithet. "He is defined by His abilities. Omnipotence, for example."

"Yes. Yes! God's abilities define Him—and *all-powerful* is the perfect place to start. What does omnipotent mean in this context?"

"It means there's nothing God can't do."

"There's nothing God can't do," Gabriel repeated. "Very well. Do we agree that God is, and in fact must be, omnipotent?"

Leonardo bit back an impulsive affirmative. "Omnipotence is an incredibly simple term for an infinitely complex topic. But I suppose there's no way around such shortcuts. I would agree that God must, at the very least, be more powerful than anything else."

"An astute clarification. I appreciate your attention to detail."

While Leonardo watched in wonder, Gabriel snapped his fingers and a stone tablet appeared. It hovered by his side, with *Omnipotent* freshly chiseled at the top. "We have our first premise. *God and only God is omnipotent.* What else?"

"Omniscient."

"All knowing," Gabriel affirmed. "That's the easy one. Easy to understand. Easy to imagine. Must God know everything?"

"Same situation as omnipotent, I believe. God must, at the very least, be more knowledgeable than anything else."

"Agreed." Gabriel snapped a second time and Omniscient appeared beneath Omnipotent on the tablet. Premise number two.

"Now, I note that you've twice said 'more than any*thing* else,' rather than 'any*one* else.' Why is that?"

Leonardo hadn't done so consciously. He paused to consider his semantic selection. "Instinct, I suppose. It's something I've pondered while painting. I've drawn scores of angels, but never God. If you think about it, He is surely not confined to flesh. If He were, He couldn't be omnipresent. And *omnipresence* undoubtedly belongs on our list."

"An enlightened answer. And you're right. Omnipresent is indeed on our list." With a wave of Gabriel's hand, the eleven letters of Omnipresent appeared beneath Omniscient. "What excites me most is the way you arrived at that conclusion. With that single shrewd observation, you have justified my faith in your abilities."

Leonardo wasn't sure where this was going, but so far he was enjoying the ride.

"As you noted a second ago, God is not corporeal," Gabriel continued. "He couldn't possibly be. Not if He is to be *everywhere*. You can't hear *everything* with a fleshy ear or see *everything* with a lidded eye. But most people maintain that preconceived picture.

Religions instill it with talk of *God making man in His image*. It's one of many misperceptions that propagate when men pretend to speak for God."

Leonardo had not considered Scripture or sermons from that angle before. *Men pretending to speak for God*. He found it disconcerting.

Gabriel picked up on his unease. "Men take mental shortcuts out of necessity. Both in seeking to understand and when trying to explain. It's infinitely easier and exponentially more comfortable to think of God as a wizened old man with a white robe and a mighty wand than as a faceless force. Unfortunately, it's that very shortcut that prevents humans from understanding Him."

"Really? That one thing?

"It's the lynchpin that locks poor assumptions in place. Hard as it may be, if you wish to succeed in this quest, you must expel that wizened-old-man image from your mind. To gain the grand unifying insight that reconciles everything you know about God, you have to start with a blank slate." Gabriel gestured toward the floating tablet. "One displaying nothing but the qualities we determine to be defining. Can you do that?"

"I can try."

Gabriel spread his wings. "Begin by understanding that I am not corporeal. Within your slumbering mind I appear in the artistic convention of an angel, but of course you cannot touch me. I have no flesh, no bone. My appearance is but a peg you use to anchor your thoughts."

An apt analogy, Leonardo thought. He would undoubtedly use it in other intellectual endeavors. Meanwhile, the insight provoked a more pressing question. "How should I think of you—if not hovering there with your halo and wings?"

"Think of me as a force, rather than an object. Like hope or magnetism or sunlight."

"A force," Leonardo repeated. "I'll try to make that mental shift. But please continue to present as I see you now. I would feel funny talking to an empty room."

"As you do when you pray?" Gabriel said with a smile.

"Good point. But during prayer, the empty room doesn't talk back."

Gabriel shimmered into a state of translucence.

"A fair compromise," Leonardo said, sincerely.

"Good. Try to begin adapting your mental image of God as well. See him as a force, rather than a flowing robe. An Omnipotent, Omniscient, Omnipresent force."

"You've repeated that a couple of times now."

"I sense subconscious resistance. A lifetime of false impressions is difficult to overcome—even with logic that's ironclad."

Leonardo believed he was mentally flexible enough to bend beneath logic regardless of prior conditioning, but he kept the arrogant assertion to himself.

Gabriel turned toward his tablet. "With Omnipotence, Omniscience and Omnipresence, we have a complete listing of God's defining *abilities*. Now we will move on to the *characteristics* and *actions* that define Him."

"Characteristics and actions," Leonardo repeated, getting a feel for the words as they rolled off his tongue.

"Yes, like the *abilities* there will be three of each. Three *abilities*, three *characteristics*, and three *actions*, bringing our total to nine."

"But there are ten spaces on the tablet," Leonardo added quizzically.

"Leave it to your artist's eye. Yes, the tenth is—" Gabriel vanished mid-sentence as a sharp pain struck Leonardo's ear.

Gioffre

Leonardo's hand flew to his aching ear as his eyes sprang open.

Prior Gioffre stared back with the same thunderous look he wielded while delivering his fire-and-brimstone sermons.

"Did you just flick my ear?" the artist asked.

"Did you really fall asleep on the job? Yet again? Even after Duke Sforza made his wishes clear?"

Gioffre had just dealt a setback to his own cause, but Leonardo couldn't begin to explain his means or methods to the shortsighted monk. So rather than fight to gain ground on infertile land, Leonardo ignored his antagonist. Without further word, he swung his legs off the boards, descended the scaffolding, and walked out of the convent—ignoring the prior's screams the whole way.

In the courtyard, Leonardo calmly mounted Euclid, kicked his heels and rode for the ghetto favored by gamblers and prostitutes.

He would find his Judas.

Or rather, the devious disciple's features. The proper purse of the lips. The perfect squint of the eyes. The nose that hinted at treachery and the brow that telegraphed underhanded intent. The set of the shoulders, the shape of the hands, the gestures and the garb. He resolved not to leave until he had catalogued everything required for the perfect portrayal.

Leonardo didn't get to the ghetto. He didn't even make it out of the high district.

"Da Vinci!"

The cry was a friendly hail rather than a hostile command. Leonardo tugged Euclid's reins and turned toward the source of the sound, a hotel he had just passed.

"Up here!"

Raising his gaze, Leonardo saw Niccolò Machiavelli standing on a balcony, cup in hand.

"Come join me for a swallow of wine."

Although Leonardo was eager to find his Judas and finish his task, the offer was tempting. While Niccolò teased him by taking a sip, Leonardo concluded that a second session with Italy's foremost master of politics and philosophy might prove productive. In any case, a few minutes of intellectual banter would help wash away the peevish prior's taint.

Leonardo hitched Euclid with a loving pat and left him with an apple. He made his way to the second-floor suite where he found the door wide open. "I thought you stayed at Bella's when visiting Milan?"

"I do. Alas, her brother is in town with his new bride. Bella has given them my usual room. But I still take most of my meals at the Blackbird, lest she think I took offense and forsake me in the future."

The stream of psychological insights that sprang from Machiavelli never ceased to amuse or astound Leonardo. "Do you ever act without strategic intent?"

Niccolò studied Leonardo's expression. "It's wise to anticipate that one's every action will be interpreted by an insecure mind."

Interpreted by an insecure mind. Leonardo liked the pragmatic turn of phrase. He found it succinct and insightful. "At this moment, I must agree."

They walked back to the balcony, where Niccolò poured a second cup from a clay pitcher. "If I'm not mistaken, even though the sun has not set since our last meeting, you've nonetheless been blessed by another visit from your celestial sponsor?"

Leonardo accepted the cup with a gracious nod. "I didn't know I was so transparent. You're right. I took a nap."

"There's little I love more than a good siesta, even when angels don't visit. Do tell."

Leonardo recounted his second session.

"Prior Gioffre literally flicked your ear, like you were a novice monk snoozing at midnight matins?" Niccolò asked.

"He really did. But let's not waste words

on him. What do you think of Gabriel's latest revelations?"

"I like his blank slate approach. If you want a revolutionary new construction, it's best not to build on an ancient foundation. And discarding the wizened old man image sounds like a sensible start. It's obvious once you think about it—the fact that He can't be physical—but I'll be the first to admit that I never challenged that notion. The white beard and flowing robe comes so naturally."

Leonardo appreciated the affirmation. "I've been thinking about that too. It's conditioned into us. The visual extension of the oft repeated verse, *Our Heavenly Father.*"

"Plus there's no ready replacement image," Niccolò added. "No alternative peg on which to anchor your thoughts."

"Quite true. How does one properly picture a force? The answer is: you can't. Forces are invisible. As a painter, I'm stuck with symbolism."

"Which brings you back to the wizened man, and reinforces the vicious circle."

"Exactly."

Both men swirled their wine before sipping. A Tuscan variety, if Leonardo wasn't mistaken. He leaned against the balcony rail and asked, "Any other observations?"

"Omnipotent, omniscient and omnipresent seem to me like the only defining qualities you need. Introduce me to the *force* that's all of those and I'll happily kneel, no further questions asked."

"The tablet has seven more spaces," Leonardo said.

"Yes, the defining characteristics and actions, plus a mysterious tenth. Those should be interesting." Niccolò gave Leonardo a funny look. "We're talking as though it really is a heavenly messenger visiting your dreams, rather than your unfettered, subconscious mind."

"I know. I've considered that too. Perhaps there's really no difference. Certainly not a practical one."

Niccolò shook his head in wonder. "You do have an amazing mind."

Leonardo finished his wine. "I'm on my

way to the ghetto to find the face of Judas. Would you care to join me?"

"I'd love to, but I'm to meet with the Duke of Bourbon in an hour. I do, however, have one suggestion before you go."

"I'm all ears."

"Take it easy on the wine this evening. We don't want that subconscious mind of yours spinning if Gabriel does come calling."

Characteristics

Leonardo saw plenty of shifty characters making sneaky moves during the six hours he spent surveying the ghetto. But nothing struck him as approaching what Judas did to Christ.

That was the rub.

What Judas did went beyond everyday treachery. It surpassed those popular peccadillos on every scale. Judas betrayed trust. And not just any trust, the trust of a friend. And not just any friend, a supremely kind-hearted friend. And not for just any reason, for the basest of reasons. For money.

As Leonardo pondered his predicament over rolls stuffed with spiced cabbage, he became ever more discouraged. To accurately observe similar skullduggery, he needed knowledge of the men involved—and their relationships. Unfortunately, any attempt to ascertain that information would disrupt the very event he was trying to observe.

Thoroughly disheartened by the time he finished his meal, Leonardo concluded that he had no choice but to improvise. Estimate. Take his best shot.

With a heavy heart, he abandoned the ghetto. He returned to his scaffold and attempted to extrapolate from what he'd observed.

Once again, try as he might, Leonardo couldn't bring himself to brush the first stroke. He wanted perfection, but perfection without example required inspiration—and he had none.

Not at that moment.

His eye fell upon a ripe red apple that Francesco had left beside the clean brushes and rags. Tempted, he tried munching and meditating, but the fruit proved ordinary, not the miraculous sort.

Eventually, Leonardo drifted off. Gabriel

soon appeared, aglow in all his glory, bathing the dreamer in a warm wave of relief.

"We were interrupted last time," the angel said.

"We were. Rather rudely."

"Perhaps there was a reason for that," Gabriel suggested.

Perhaps there was, but Leonardo didn't care to dwell on it. He wanted to use his precious time with Gabriel discussing God, not Gioffre.

Sensing as much, Gabriel dove right in. "We were about to embark on a discussion of God's *characteristics*. Three qualities that are central to His identity. Can you think of one?"

Although not an overtly religious man, Leonardo considered himself spiritual. He was also intimately familiar with the Bible. Detailed knowledge informed his work and satisfied his natural curiosity. Furthermore, he had attended scores of worship services and overheard countless theological discussions and prayers while working on *The Last Supper*.

Reflecting on those experiences in light of Gabriel's question, a couple of common refrains came quickly to mind: *our eternal Father*, and *the everlasting Lord*. "God is eternal."

Gabriel grinned and *Eternal* appeared on the tablet. "Excellent. Now give me two more."

Motivated and excited though he was, Leonardo drew a blank.

"Don't overthink it," Gabriel urged. "What is the characteristic that binds God with religion?"

The clue didn't help.

It wasn't until Gabriel brought his palms together in a familiar pose that Leonardo understood. It took him another moment to properly formulate prayer as a defining characteristic. "God is *worthy of worship*."

"Precisely!" With a wave the words appeared in stone, filling the fifth line. "*Worthy of worship* is particularly important, for it is the practical characteristic. It's the one that translates into daily action for the enlightened mind."

"The enlightened mind being the one that comprehends God?"

"Correct."

"I'm afraid I don't follow."

Repeating a now familiar refrain, Gabriel said, "I know. But you will." He gestured back toward the tablet. "We need one more."

A force, rather than a flowing robe. Omnipotent, omniscient, omnipresent, eternal, worthy of worship, and something else. Leonardo's mind darted this way and that without yielding anything compelling—until he dredged up his first interactions with the Almighty.

He remembered a small stone home on a hillside in Venci, and the cozy kitchen within. He saw his young self seated with clasped hands and bowed head before a bowl of soup at a worn wooden supper table. *God is great, God is good...* "My impulse is to add *benevolent*, but I'm not certain that's entirely appropriate."

"Why not?" Gabriel prodded with repressed expression.

"It is my experience that whether or not something is benevolent is often a question of perspective. Frogs may be grateful to a benevolent God for the insects they eat, but flies will have an entirely different point of view."

"Outstanding!" Gabriel's halo expanded to twice its normal size and luster. Clearly, he was very excited. "With that single, simple observation, eloquently presented, you've shown more insight into the essence of God than the vast majority of religious scholars." Gabriel snapped his fingers and added *Benevolent* to the tablet.

"I don't understand," Leonardo said. "What insight? Why did you add benevolent?"

"When it comes to comprehending God, most men who possess the intellect to question fail to do so from a universal point of view. They remain trapped in their own perspective, considering the individual rather than the collective. The piece rather than the whole."

Leonardo wasn't certain that he followed, so he decided to test his understanding. "Is it like taxes? Where the cost is clear and immediate but the benefits are abstract and distant?"

"That's an original analogy, astute and appropriate, but it doesn't capture the typical tripping point. Most people aren't so sophisticated."

Leonardo took a second to reassess. "People can't get past how God can let anything bad happen to them or those they love."

"Exactly. The problem is having an omnipotent, benevolent god coexist with acts of evil. Philosophers have been debating this apparent contradiction for ages."

"Is there a satisfactory solution?"

Gabriel spread his arms in a reassuring gesture. "The cleanest way to address that conflict is to continue on our course. For now, please have faith that once you understand God, you will know that despite the existence of evil, He is truly both benevolent and omnipotent."

Leonardo felt shorted.

"You don't appear comfortable with my promise."

Leonardo wasn't sure what tack to take in answering. On the one hand, this was his dream. On the other, he was addressing the Archangel Gabriel. "I am skeptical, but hopeful and ever eager to learn."

"I would expect nothing less. It is because of those very qualities that I believe our quest will succeed."

"One more clarification, if I may?"

"Quickly. We are running short on time."

Indeed they were. Before Leonardo could voice his question, his vision vanished. This unfortunate turn of events evoked another question, one he'd often wanted to ask the Almighty. *Why had He designed a bladder that could not last the whole night?*

Actions

Leonardo managed the maneuver everyone hopes for when the call of nature disrupts their slumber. Despite having to descend and later ascend twenty-five feet of scaffolding, and even though he had to traipse across a cold courtyard to a malodorous outhouse, he still fell back asleep within seconds of resuming a horizontal position.

The dream soon followed.

Gabriel wasted no time. He turned toward his tablet with an enthusiastic sweep of his arm. "We've discussed the *abilities* and *characteristics* that define God. To complete the picture, we must also cover God's *actions*.

"While Scripture and practice vary widely from one religion to the next, there are three defining activities that the major monotheistic religions all assign to God. Each is the topic of many a philosophical treatise. Can you guess what they are?"

Leonardo's ear latched onto the word *philosophical*. No doubt as Gabriel intended. Philosophical led to philosopher and the first idea followed. "Aristotle's *Unmoved Mover* leaps to mind."

"Excellent. Yes. God started everything. He was the first force in the universe. The impetus of all action."

"The impetus of all action," Leonardo repeated, finding the phrase delightfully descriptive.

After chiseling *Unmoved Mover* on the tablet, Gabriel asked, "What else?"

Leonardo was ready. "God as *creator* follows like left foot after right."

"Indeed it does. God created the universe and all that is in it."

Creator appeared on the tablet.

What a staggering accomplishment. Leonardo hadn't really dwelled on the enormity of creation until that very moment. If everything was truly created by just one—he almost said *man*—force, what an awesome force He must be. Powerful enough to have rendered not just the birds and the bees, but the very sky in which they flew.

Despite their rapid progress, Gabriel did not give Leonardo time to dwell on past revelations. He pushed forward as though they were short on time. "Just one more action to go. To speed things up, I'll give you a hint as to its nature. This one is ongoing."

Leonardo drew a blank.

Gabriel prompted him further. "What is it that most men of faith fear? Particularly the wicked."

Of course! "Judgment. God judges."

"Indeed He does!" The word *Judge* appeared, completing the triple trinity with three abilities, three characteristics, and three actions. Only the tablet's mysterious tenth position remained blank.

Eager though he was to lift that last curtain, Leonardo held up a finger. "There's something about the idea of judgment that has always bothered me. If I might ask?"

"I am at your service."

"I'm puzzled by what it means for God to judge *all* things. The church would have us believe that the righteous go to Heaven and the wicked go to Hell, but that's a single, binary decision. And it seems contradictory to the fundamental idea that God judges *all* things."

"Go on," Gabriel prompted.

"People take millions of consequential actions in their lives. Some are good, some are bad. A man might save a child's life one day and kill a child the next. In sum, he might do a million good deeds, and a million and one bad. While another might do a million and one good, and a million bad. To give one man an eternity of Heaven and the other everlasting Hell for essentially the same score does not strike me as just."

"How does it strike you?" Gabriel asked, his tone more inquisitive than accusatory.

"It strikes me as a crude and uninspired shortcut."

Gabriel stroked the side of the tablet with a long, fine finger. "You began by saying *the church would have us believe.* Churches are no different from other institutions. In order to connect with the masses, they must simplify things to a level low enough that everyone can comprehend. Scholars and shepherds. Princes and paupers.

"Heaven and Hell are concepts that even modest minds can grasp. The same can be said of a single day of judgment following one's death. This inherent need to simplify ideas enough to make them digestible by every patron is another reason why you would be better served by disregarding doctrine for the purposes of our discussion."

Leonardo approved of the logic and appreciated the practicality. He found himself furthering Gabriel's line of reasoning. "Such a simplistic scheme clearly serves the church's self-interest. It both expands and energizes their business base. Fear of Hell's fires puts a lot of people in pews."

"It certainly does. I'm pleased to see your perspective evolving."

Satisfied with their progress but eager to

unveil the penultimate mystery, Leonardo gestured toward the tablet. "We still have one space to go."

"Yes, and no," Gabriel said, surprising the sleeping artist. "The last position is not for a defining quality. Our list is already complete. Three abilities, three characteristics, three actions. The tenth space is a placeholder. A reminder."

Now Leonardo was truly perplexed.

"I added that space to draw attention to a serious *misperception*. A mental roadblock. A barrier we must lift with logic before we proceed."

Leonardo pushed back. "I believe that I've demonstrated an exceptionally open mind."

"In comparison to most others, you certainly have," Gabriel said with a sympathetic smile. "But I assure you that bias burns bright within you nonetheless. Exceptionally open is not the same as entirely open. Like everyone else, you have been conditioned. A lifetime of repetition has led you to embrace a false proposition. To internalize a sticky misperception."

Leonardo hadn't a clue where this was headed. *He had been conditioned? Through a lifetime of repetition?* "Try though I might, I can't guess where you're going."

"This particular bit of misinformation is so inconspicuous and common that you and I have each repeated it a dozen times during our discussions."

Gabriel paused a beat to allow his revelation to sink in. Only when Leonardo met his eye did he continue. "The incorrect assumption is so deeply ingrained that switching away from it will feel like diverting the flow of a mighty river. No matter how hard you struggle, the current will fight you. But if you wish to become enlightened, you must swim through to the other side. I say this even though logic will convince you that the conclusion is unquestionably correct."

Now Leonardo was completely flummoxed. *What assumption could cause him to forgo logic?* He felt his pulse quicken and had to work to calm it, lest he waken. "You've got me more curious than I've ever been in my life. Both to see the method you'll use, and for the big reveal."

"Glad I've got your full attention. That's no mean feat, given that you're sleeping," Gabriel added with a wink. "We'll use the Socratic approach. I will guide you with questions, the first being this. Do you agree that precision is an important part of our analysis?"

"Yes, of course."

"And imprecision could taint our ultimate conclusion?"

"Most certainly."

"So social conventions, where imprecise, would best be avoided. Do you agree?"

Leonardo still had no idea where this was going. "Agreed."

Gabriel pressed his fingertips together. "Thank you. Now answer me this: *Does God reproduce?*"

Rather than dwell on the bizarre question, Leonardo dove straight into the analysis. Speaking to himself, he said, "Christians consider Jesus to be the son of God, and Scripture indicates that we're all God's children. But neither Jesus nor any other man is omnipotent, omniscient, or omnipresent. So I would conclude that God has not reproduced. Not literally.

"Furthermore, logic dictates that there can only be one omnipotent force." Leonardo looked up at Gabriel. "No. There is only one God. He does not reproduce."

The set of Gabriel's mouth and the crease of his eyes indicated that Leonardo had answered properly, but rather than confirming this, Gabriel probed further. "So God is asexual, biologically speaking? Without gender?"

It was a question that Leonardo had never thought to ask, even though it was the type of problem he loved to ponder.

He'd just deduced that God had not reproduced. And earlier, during the discussion of omnipresence, they had concluded that God was not a physical entity. Therefore, it followed that He did not have genitalia—or any other physical manifestation for that matter. "Yes, as odd as it sounds to say, it would be more proper than not to consider Him asexual. Without gender."

"Indeed it would. We are almost there."

Leonardo found himself squirming as Gabriel spoke. Their conversation had become uncomfortable.

"One last question. Given the importance that precision plays in our analysis, and the fact that God has no gender, should we not refer to God as *It*, rather than *Him*?"

Leonardo felt his jaw drop. From his biological studies, he knew exactly which muscles had relaxed. Their names leapt unbidden to his mind. The temporalis and masseter muscles. Both remained limp as overcooked spaghetti.

"That's all we have time for," Gabriel exclaimed. "I believe you have plenty to puzzle over while awake."

Leonardo was about to protest when a chorus of voices burst forth all around him. His eyes popped open and he rolled toward the source of the sound, nearly plummeting from the scaffolding in the process.

The refectory was ablaze with the light of a hundred candles, and awash in the sound of singing monks. To pressure Leonardo to complete the Lord's work, Prior Gioffre had moved 3 a.m. matins to the refectory.

Once again, the misguided monk had chased off Leonardo's inspiring angel.

Judas

Leonardo slid his legs around and sat up in the reverse of his usual position, facing the refectory rather than the mural wall. He studied the singing monks while shucking off sleep. They had arranged themselves behind and around the dining tables. The swarthy Prior stood alone in the center like the axis around which the lesser brothers spun.

Leonardo locked his gaze on Gioffre. The leader's eyes were defiant. Taunting even. Emboldened by the duke's intervention and the coming of the King, his blazing brown irises seemed to scream *See me here in all my power! I am the left hand of the Lord. How dare you defy me.*

Refusing to look away, Leonardo stared

right back. Then, as he strained not to blink, it struck.

The insight.

The inspiration.

Without further thought or a second glance, he lifted his legs and rotated back around, presenting his back to the pesky prior.

With the chorus continuing its haunting harmonies and the hundred handheld candles providing plenty of light, Leonardo began painting. The hawk-like nose, the crinkled face, the pursed lips, the defiant jaw. Eyes screaming self-righteousness above a bare lip and a bedraggled beard.

He worked with a passion and a fervor he had not felt in months. He worked without noticing when the sun rose or the monks left or the refectory resumed its normal daily business. He worked until the face and chest and hands were perfect. He worked until *The Last Supper* had its Judas.

"Perfect!"

While enjoying the sense of satisfaction achieved by killing two birds with one stone,

Leonardo summoned Francesco to clean his brushes. His young assistant did a double take upon seeing the new development. "Is that who I think it is?"

"Did I leave room for doubt or confusion?"

Francesco shrugged. "There's no mistaking either the face or the expression. I just hadn't expected to see either immortalized."

Leonardo couldn't help deriving a sense of satisfaction from his assistant's mixed expression. "I doubt you'll be the only one. I'm off to breakfast."

Leonardo left without looking back.

Twenty minutes later, he found Niccolò at the Blackbird Tavern eating soft boiled eggs and pomegranate. The politician was seated between two ladies. Leonardo couldn't tell whether they were working girls or would-be wives. This close to the castle, everyone was upper-crust.

Niccolò dismissed his companions promptly but politely as Leonardo approached. No money changed hands.

He then motioned toward the same warm

seat Leonardo had occupied two days earlier. "Last night's lesson must have been something special. I don't recall ever seeing your face so animated."

"It was a very special night. I found Judas—right beneath my nose. Gabriel and I also had our most fascinating discussion yet."

"Do tell."

"It was the first time the archangel revealed something utterly surprising. Almost makes me wonder if he exists only in my mind."

"Now you've really got me intrigued."

Leonardo motioned for the waiter to bring him the same breakfast as Niccolò, then resumed his story. "In our earlier discussions, Gabriel and I covered the blank-slate, bottoms-up methodology we're using to get to God. We also talked through His defining attributes. The closest we got to anything controversial was pointing out an obvious conclusion that isn't often drawn."

"Namely?"

"That God is not flesh and blood."

"Yes, we discussed that yesterday. Go on," Niccolò urged, his expression intense.

"Last night, Gabriel took that lesson one giant leap further. He pointed out that given God's lack of physical embodiment or reproductive function, the proper pronoun for the Almighty is *It,* not *Him*."

Niccolò's eyes widened as if a stiletto had skewered his liver. But he didn't blurt out a reflexive denial or attempt a refutation. He just blinked a few times before taking another bite of egg. After much chewing and an exaggerated swallow, he said, "I can't deny the logic, but I can tell you one thing for certain. You'll never work for the church again if you ever repeat that conclusion."

Revelation

Given his controversial rendering of Judas, Leonardo concluded that he would be wise to avoid the monks and patrons of Santa Maria delle Grazie until he was prepared to paint Jesus. To avoid any such encounter, he rode Euclid thirty minutes north of the Blackbird Tavern and spent the day walking in the woods while contemplating Gabriel's revelations and Niccolò's observations.

Da Vinci found it hard to wrap his head around the fact that he had a meeting pending with the Almighty. *Might it actually happen? What would it be like?* The answers were maddeningly impossible to predict. But rather than follow in Saint Jerome's footsteps and beat himself with a rock, Leonardo wandered the woods in search of tranquility and wisdom.

Late in the day, while riding for home all dirty and disheveled, Da Vinci realized that he ought to be preparing his body as well as his mind. Inspired by the idea but unwilling to waste mental energy on mundane tasks, he found a bathhouse far from the church.

When he emerged an hour later, his hair was washed, his body perfumed, and his face clean shaven. By the time he stood beside his large four-poster bed, both his body and mind were set for slumber—and anything else that might occur. That was when Leonardo realized his mistake. Gabriel had only visited him on church grounds. Specifically, while he was sleeping on scaffolding.

Unwilling to risk breaking the cycle, Leonardo arose, redressed and returned to Santa Maria delle Grazie.

"Thank goodness you're back," Leonardo said as Gabriel appeared. "I feared that our earlier interactions, like so many dreams, would prove to be a tease."

Gabriel's eyes lost focus and his mouth

turned down. He'd been wounded.

Leonardo quickly backpedaled. "What I mean is, this has become very important to me. If for any reason I'm unable to complete what we've begun, I fear it will distract me for the rest of my days. Coming so close to the ultimate answer but failing to acquire it might even prove maddening."

Instead of quipping about Leonardo's lack of faith, Gabriel said, "I'm an angel. We try not to disappoint."

"Of course. I know that. It's just my nature to worry when I care so strongly."

Gabriel spread his arms. "You and I have come a long way, Leonardo. I am confident that tonight our journey will reach its glorious conclusion. Let us begin our last hours together by reflecting on prior learnings."

Leonardo felt a lump forming in his throat. "Very well."

"We began by picturing a force, rather than a flowing robe. We ended by determining that the asexual *It* is a more proper pronoun for God than the conventional *He.*

"During our intervening discussions we agreed on the triple trinity of qualities that define God and only God. Those nine descriptors are our premises, and they are chiseled in stone." Gabriel gestured toward the hovering tablet.

"We identified God as *omnipotent, omniscient and omnipresent. It* is the *unmoved mover* who *created* the universe and *judges* our actions. *It* is *benevolent, eternal,* and *worthy of worship.*"

Leonardo couldn't help but interject. "That pronoun pesters like a pebble in the shoe."

Gabriel dismissed the gripe with a wave of the wrist. "The discomfort will soon pass, I assure you. And speaking of comforts, are you content with our list of premises? Confident that we didn't miss a defining requirement?"

Leonardo shared a thought that had come to him in the bath. "I considered adding *infallible.* That's a term priests like to toss around. But I discarded it."

"And why is that?"

"Humans aren't poised to judge matters from God's perspective, so how can we say what is or is not a mistake? To my eye, the world is full of apparent imperfections. In fact, I might argue that it has no perfections."

"Good point. Perfection is a matter of perspective." Gabriel gestured as he spoke, conducting an invisible orchestra with fingers and palms. "Is there a perfect food? No. The perfection of a balanced diet can only be achieved through variety. So it is with most things. But variety requires variance, which by definition is imperfection.

"It is only when you consider God's creation as a whole that you can understand its *grand perfection*. While that comprehensive grasp is beyond even your great mind, the concept is readily within your reach. You demonstrated as much with your frog and fly analogy."

"Thank you. Does that mean *infallibility* is like *benevolence*?"

"It is in the regard that evaluating it requires the complete context. But since that universal perspective is beyond human ability, I think you'll concur that it would be counterproductive to add *infallibility* to our list."

"Agreed."

"So again I ask you, are we happy with our nine? When I present the persona that pulls our defining qualities into a tight and tidy bundle, will you concede that you must be gazing upon God—regardless of the novelty and clash with conventional descriptions?"

Leonardo found that an odd question. He thought the insight would be so blindingly obvious as to be unquestionable. "Why do you ask?"

"I ask because you are a man who lives among men. Not just men, but men of the church. The sermons, the Scriptures, the images they put in your head, all those impact your ability to approach God without preconceived notions.

"We agreed early on that you had to enter our discussion with a completely open mind. A blank slate. Ideally, you will now consider nothing but the nine qualities on our tablet, while keeping in mind our tenth understanding. But that is easier said than done. In fact, it is impossible. Still, with a mind as pure and analytical as yours, I believe it's worth a try."

Worth a try? Leonardo felt panic well within him. The overwhelming fear of pending loss.

He had been expecting Gabriel to present him with the grand unifying insight. A gift on a silver platter. Now he understood that it would not be so simple. *Could not* be so simple, he corrected. If it were, someone would have figured it out long ago.

With that thought weighing heavily on his heart, the genius of Gabriel's tactic struck him like a bolt from a blue sky, providing energy and clarity. The tablet was the key. The tool Leonardo could use to set aside his prejudices and preconceived notions. All he had to do was focus on the nine properties now set in stone as if they were the components of a mathematical equation.

When working math problems, you didn't introduce extraneous variables. You used the parameters provided. Since Leonardo had personally approved each element of the equation, he felt confident that he could in fact embrace the logical conclusion to which they led.

That tactic was exactly what Gabriel had initially suggested. He looked up at the angel. "Time to solve for God."

"Yes it is."

Despite all the buildup, Leonardo had trouble believing that there existed a grand unifying insight that would reconcile faith with reason. A logical pathway to the Almighty.

"Will it surprise you to learn that you have known God all along? Wholly and completely?"

Yes! It will. "I don't understand."

"You know God. Intimately if not perfectly. As, of course, you must if you think about it—since by definition God is always with you."

"How is that possible?" Leonardo asked.

"God hides in plain sight, camouflaged like a king in monk's garb. It does this by wearing another name. You know God as *time*."

Arguments

After the big revelation, Leonardo expected Gabriel to fade away, but the archangel remained fully lit and center stage. That too was a blessing, as Leonardo had questions screaming for answers.

He blurted out the first one that came to mind. "But time is—" He paused, unable to properly complete the sentence.

"What?" Gabriel asked with the hint of a mischievous smile. "Not a wizened old man with a white robe and a mighty wand?"

Leonardo felt foolish.

But only for a second.

"Time is not animate."

Gabriel's smile faded. "You want to add *Animate* to our list?"

Leonardo felt like a cheater, and his

words came out correspondingly weak. "It's just assumed."

Gabriel's tone remained forceful and steady. "Perhaps that assumption is the primary problem. The blind spot that prevents people from seeing the truth."

"Are you implying that God is not animate?"

Gabriel's gaze didn't waiver. "Answer me this: What do you mean by animate?"

"Alive."

"Define alive—in a way that's not circular."

Leonardo didn't have a ready answer. After struggling through a few false starts, the best he could come up with was, "Not dead."

"And I suppose you'll define dead as *not alive?*"

Leonardo saw the archangel's point. Odd that he hadn't considered that circularity on prior occasion.

Gabriel continued. "If you try to define *alive* without creating a circular reference, and you bear in mind that plants, for example, are alive, you'll likely end up with something like: *Still in existence, force, or operation.* Does that sound accurate to you?"

"It does."

"Good. Now tell me this: Does that definition apply to time?"

Leonardo guessed that this was what it felt like to be one of Socrates' students, led to obvious conclusions by obscure questions—with one's intellectual inferiority on constant display. "Time's existence, force and operation are all evidenced by our every action. By this very discussion. This is so weird."

"Answer the question."

"Yes. Time does indeed fit that definition of animate."

Gabriel didn't rest on his laurels. "Alternatively, you might define animate as *Marked by alertness, energy, animation or activity.*"

Leonardo liked that definition. It was closer to what he initially had in mind. "Yes, that sounds better. It feels right too."

"Good. Then answer me this: How would you know whether any of those defining characteristics was exhibited by an *incorporeal* entity—as we've repeatedly determined that God must be?"

"Huh," was all Leonardo managed to say. He felt blindsided once again. He had literally proven his powers of observation to be second to none by creating descriptive accounts of beating bird and insect wings. But Gabriel had stumped him. *How could you observe alertness, energy, animation, or activity in God—given that It had no physical presence?*

He began thinking out loud. "Well, *direct* observation is out, since by definition we can't see that which is incorporeal. Although" —he corrected himself with a sense of excitement, "light and shadow are exceptions, so there may be others."

"Let me know if you think of any." Gabriel's tone revealed the inevitable conclusion to that quest. "Meanwhile, keep going."

"That leaves us with only *indirect* observation."

"Exactly. And—" Gabriel held up a finger for emphasis, "*indirect* is in fact how everyone describes observations of God, right? Outside of dreams and visions, nobody has credibly claimed to see or hear or touch God for over a thousand years."

"I can't argue with that," Leonardo said.

"What people do see, hear and touch are the *results* of actions. Results that the faithful ascribe to God, but nonbelievers attribute to chance instead."

Leonardo felt the first inkling of acceptance warming the back of his brain. "A fair point."

"Of course, God's causation cannot be scientifically verified. If so, there would be no nonbelievers. That's why they call it faith." Gabriel pointed to his tablet. "Therefore, with both direct and indirect confirmation impossible, it would be pointless to include *Animate* on our list."

"Wow. Indeed it would." Again Leonardo had not seen a conclusion coming.

"I know you're still struggling, and I understand. The wizened old man is a stubborn image. He's very difficult to dislodge."

As Leonardo let the implications sink in, another inference followed like the left foot after the right. He turned back to his teacher. "Anyone who believes in God must take the Almighty's animation on faith."

Gabriel graciously nodded. "Indeed they must."

Leonardo got the feeling that Gabriel was saddling another unbroken horse for a wild ride.

"Answer me this," the archangel continued. "How do you define time—in a noncircular way?"

Given his earlier experience, Leonardo did not rush to answer. He spoke up only after reaching a comfortable conclusion. "Time is a measurement of existence."

"Very good. That's an excellent conventional definition. But—as you are about to see—it is only a partial definition."

"Apparently so," Leonardo said, thinking about the list chiseled in stone.

"Are you familiar with the fable of the four blindfolded men and the elephant?"

Leonardo snugged his boots in the

metaphorical stirrups. "Kindly remind me."

"Four blindfolded men are led into a room that contains an elephant. One has his hands placed on the tail, another on the trunk, the third on an ear, and the fourth on a tusk. Each is told that he is touching an elephant, and is asked to describe the animal to the others from where he stands."

"And each describes an entirely different beast," Leonardo interjected. "They argue with passion and verve about what an elephant is, each certain of his description because of what he feels with his own hands. Then the blindfolds are removed and each sees how shortsighted he has been. I remember now."

Gabriel raised both index fingers. "To get at the truth, you often need to move beyond the apparent answer. The obvious conclusion. You need to be willing to abandon your current, comfortable footing and reach for the unknown. Keep that in mind as we return to our discussion."

"I shall."

"If you think about it, time is clearly much

more than *a measurement of existence.* Marks on a ledger and ticks on a clock are just the hairs of time's tail. You are about to see that time is—and in fact *must* also be—a force."

"I am thinking about it," Leonardo said. "And it's not clear at all."

"That's because I haven't removed your blindfold yet."

"And how does one remove a metaphorical blindfold?" Leonardo asked.

"With the right question."

"And what question is that?"

Gabriel spread his arms and raised his wings as his halo began to pulse with golden light. "What is left of the world, if you take away time?"

———

Leonardo awoke but did not rise. He lay with his back on the boards and his cloak wrapped tightly, contemplating Gabriel's crowning question. *What is left of the world, if you take away time?*

Try as he might to find other avenues or

approaches, to strip or sort or stack the logic in alternative ways, he always arrived at the same conclusion. A single, simple, stark answer. *Nothing.* There was nothing without time.

Confirmation

Eager to continue their discussion to its conclusion, Leonardo closed his eyes and prayed for slumber's embrace. Given his state of intellectual arousal, the monks' midnight matins came and went before his prayer was answered.

"Do you need a review?" Gabriel said by way of greeting. Clearly he assumed that Leonardo had reached the obvious conclusion and accepted the corollary result. *Time* was indeed much more than a measurement—for without it there was nothing.

"No need for a review," Leonardo replied.

Gabriel stayed silent.

Unsure where to go next, Leonardo added, "During my reflection, I came to appreciate your elephant analogy. That visual of a closed mind—the tusks, trunk and ears beyond my reach—makes it much easier to maintain an open mind."

"Glad to hear it," Gabriel said. He tapped the tablet twice with a short staff that appeared in his hand. *Tap tap*. "Let us proceed with our original plan. Our mathematical operation. Talk yourself through the list of defining qualities—one by one. Convince yourself that *time* solves for *God*."

"You've rearranged the list," Leonardo said, focusing on it for the first time this session. "The *actions* are now on top."

"It's easy when you don't actually have to chisel," Gabriel said with a smile. "And I find the analysis flows better with the attributes listed in this order, *actions*, then *abilities*, then *characteristics*."

"Whatever you say."

Leonardo began with the first. "Is time the Unmoved Mover? In other words, did time start it all? Of course It did. By definition. Before time there was nothing. That seems so obvious now."

He looked up at Gabriel, who spoke reassuringly without further prompting. "I know. I know."

Leonardo resisted the impulse to move on immediately. "I want to dig deeper."

"By all means."

Speaking more to himself than to Gabriel, Leonardo began. "Is there anything else that could be considered to have started it all? The chemist in me is inclined to consider various forms of energy, heat or light. But neither survives even cursory scrutiny. They're entirely insufficient. All are impotent without time." As the internal calculations continued, he slowly shook his head. "The only apparent alternative is the wizened old man with a wand—which logically we know to be no alternative at all."

"Very good. Shall we move on?" Gabriel prompted.

Leonardo turned back to the precious list. "Did time *create* everything? This one feels a bit more slippery."

"Try switching your perspective," Gabriel

suggested. "Come at it from the other side."

By reversing the question, grabbing the tusks rather than the tail, Leonardo quickly found firm footing. "Is there anything without time? Well, clearly there's no movement. And without movement you can't have change. Or growth. Or life. So no, there's nothing without time. Therefore, we can conclude that time makes everything possible."

"Very good," Gabriel concurred. "Keep going. Rule out any alternative."

"Could the same be said of anything else? Was there another all-empowering force?" Try as he might, Leonardo got nowhere. "Nothing trumps time. In fact, even a wizened man with a magic wand is powerless without time."

Gabriel grew a satisfied expression. Bright eyes, raised cheeks, relaxed mouth.

Leonardo felt like he could stop there and be content with the conclusion. Intellectually and spiritually. But he pressed on—thoroughly enjoying the process now that it was flowing.

"Does time *judge*?" A few thoughts immediately entered his mind. "It is often said that *time judges all things* and *only time will tell*. But those aren't literal attributions, are they?"

"Are you asking a process question?" Gabriel pressed. "How judging is accomplished?"

"I suppose I am."

"Again, I bring you back to a fact we established early on. To be all-seeing and all-knowing, God cannot be corporeal. Just as there are no fleshy eyes and ears hovering everywhere, there is no big body of gray matter in the sky."

"Of course. Agreed."

"Given that lack of a physical repository, you must ask yourself: Where is that judgment stored? Where is it *contained?*"

The answer slipped from Leonardo's lips. "In time."

"That's right. Judgment is *contained* in time and—to answer the logical follow-on—*transmitted* by people. Through their works, words, memories and emotions."

Leonardo felt another puzzle piece snap into place. "And that's how judgment is reflected back on the actor. How God judges every notable act."

"Exactly."

Leonardo looked at the chiseled list with unbridled amazement. "The *actions* all fit. Time solves for all of them."

"Indeed it does. And time's *abilities?*"

Leonardo took a deep breath, then dove right back in. The water was warm.

"Is time Omnipotent? That answer is also cliché. Also baked into the collective conscious. Also hiding in plain sight. *All things in time. With time, all things are possible.*"

Gabriel stayed silent.

Again Leonardo dug deeper. Pressed his omnipotence analysis further. "Is there anything that time cannot accomplish?" His thoughts flew to the miracles made possible by time. "The Egyptians built buildings tall enough to touch the clouds. The Romans created artificial rivers, aqueducts that service their cities and their homes. An English friar devised lenses that fix faulty eyes. Human history is full of things that once seemed impossible but became commonplace—with time."

"Keep going," Gabriel urged.

"Is there anything that time does not make possible? As an artist, architect, and engineer, my mind goes to The Great Pyramid of Giza when I think about the impossible. Constructing it required 2.3 million limestone blocks, each weighing as much as five full-grown oxen. The Egyptians quarried, cut, measured, moved, lifted and installed twelve of those mammoth blocks every hour, day and night, for twenty years. The impossible plan became possible with time."

"Don't just look back, look forward," Gabriel suggested.

Leonardo's thoughts turned to the flying machines he had engineered on paper. While he could not prove it, he felt certain that, with time, man would even take to the sky. His mind also went to medicine, to the studies he had completed and those he had planned. Extrapolating forward, he could see disease and perhaps even death being eradicated—with time. "You are right. Nothing is more powerful than time."

Gabriel beckoned back to the list. "One ability left."

Leonardo continued to think out loud. "Omniscient. That one is self-evident. Time bears witness to everything. Not witness in the sense of a big brain putting eyeballs on events—we dismissed that silly notion earlier—but witness in the sense that every event is intertwined with time. In fact, time is a defining characteristic of every event."

"How about Omnipresent?" Gabriel asked.

"That one is even more self-evident. No place is untouched by time." Leonardo glanced at the tablet. "The further I progress down our list, the more foolish I feel for not having figured this out long ago. How could I have missed this? Half of these are so well established as to be *cliché.*"

Gabriel gave a knowing nod. "The short answer is that you've been taught to automatically ascribe these things to a wizened old man with a wand. We've been over that.

"Do you want to stop here, for now? I've already weighted down your mind and there's some heavy lifting going forward."

Conclusion

Leonardo needed no time to consider Gabriel's question. He felt more than ready for some heavy lifting. He was two-thirds of the way there with momentum at his back. Only the *characteristics* remained. "No! I want to move on. I have to say I'm amazed by how easy it was to get through the *actions* and *abilities*—given how hard it was to come up with the solution."

"We've still got God's *characteristics*," Gabriel said with a wink.

Leonardo read the next line on the list. "Benevolent. Hmmm. Benevolent is an interesting one."

"Yes, perhaps the most interesting one," Gabriel agreed.

"Conventional wisdom directly addresses

it with *time heals all wounds*. But clearly time's benevolence goes much deeper than that. Now that you have me thinking about time as a force in my life, I see that it's my most precious resource. More valuable than food, water—even love."

"As God should be. The church got that right. Time is the most important resource in our lives. In fact, it is the defining characteristic of life."

"The defining characteristic of life," Leonardo repeated. He would definitely dissect that nugget later on. For the moment he was eager to finish. Only *eternal* and *worthy of worship* remained.

"Is time *eternal?* Silly question. They're synonyms.

"Is time *worthy of worship?* The *worthy* part isn't instantly obvious, but people certainly worship time. Just ask anyone turning fifty what he wants most. And how often have I heard my elders say, *Every minute is a gift*. It's also fair to say that most of the elderly worship youth—albeit without the naivety that typically accompanies that age."

Leonardo's excitement grew as the conclusions continued to cascade. "Even children participate in their own way. They might not realize why they feel so vibrant and free, but adults know it comes from an intuitive understanding that they have plenty of time."

He circled back to the original question. "Is time *worthy* of worship? Now that answer is clear. Of course! What deserves veneration more than existence itself? More than the opportunity to—"

As Leonardo pondered the latest interesting insight, a marvelous revelation arose. "By sharing Itself with us, is time not making us gods? If not as individuals, then collectively? Are we not, as a species, omnipotent, omniscient, and benevolent? Are we not creators?"

Gabriel literally began beaming with pride. "You've just enjoyed your first glimpse of the entire elephant."

Leonardo felt a warm glow spreading within. He pressed forward. "That's what is meant by *we're all God's children* and *created in*

His image. It's not us as individuals, it's humanity as a whole. We are God's eyes and ears, arms and legs, memory and understanding. And that is why we are all equal. We are all, quite literally, at one with God."

Gabriel spread his wings in silent acknowledgment.

Leonardo's excitement erupted like Vesuvius as the conclusion cascade continued. "That's so profound, yet so simple. It squares the circle of my understanding. Suddenly, everything fits. Comfortably."

Gabriel gave Leonardo a few seconds to swallow, then said, "Very glad to hear it. Now finish your analysis."

Leonardo thought that he had finished.

Gabriel tapped the last line again.

Leonardo forced his focus back to the tablet. "Is *worthy of worship* more than just another criterion?"

Gabriel answered with a question of his own. "How is it different from the other eight?"

The clever question led Leonardo to the answer. "It's about us as much as it is about Him."

"About *It*," Gabriel corrected. "That's right. Continue."

"Given my newfound understanding of God, I will do a better job of worshiping It. I will treat time with the deference It is due."

As the words crossed his lips, Leonardo sensed that he would lead a richer, more contented life going forward. Even bad times would somehow be special now. Knowing that each minute was actually God's embrace would make every second sacred. He wouldn't want to waste a single moment.

Leonardo looked Gabriel in the eye. "You've given me a priceless gift."

Gabriel bowed. "You're welcome."

"And you were right. Now that I know the truth, the proper pronoun no longer sticks in my throat."

"Almost seems silly, doesn't it? The conventional picture of the Almighty as an old man in a white robe rather than an omnipresent force?"

"I feel as though this knowledge has lit a candle within my mind. What once was dark, now is light." Leonardo smiled at his ironic turn of biblical phrase—and woke himself up.

He lay staring up at the surrounding scaffolding. The boards above had been removed, but the uprights, ledgers and transoms remained. He ran a tender hand across the wood that had been his nest for three years.

Three years' worth of time.

Was it time well spent? Had he used his gift wisely? Was The Last Supper *a worthy investment?*

Leonardo spent several minutes studying his masterpiece, not as an artist or engineer, but as an everyday observer. He concluded that it was the most beautiful thing he had ever created.

Continuing the analysis, Da Vinci studied his work from a technical perspective. In his opinion, it was the most perfect mural ever painted. The composition, expressions and gestures he'd labored so long to perfect made it lively and compelling. The picture sucked the observer in even as the story leapt out.

Then there was the technique he'd used to manipulate perspective. It was little short of magical. Even the tempera paints were special. A first. His invention.

Yes, Leonardo decided, he had used his time wisely.

Content with that knowledge, he closed his eyes.

Jesus

Gabriel did not reappear.

Rather than rejoicing in reunion, Leonardo found himself running across an endless desert, his bare feet scorched by burning sand. With no shade in sight, he was forced to scamper in circles to keep his flesh from frying.

As often happens in unwelcome dreams, the environment evolved in a malicious manner. The sand began shifting, sinking, streaming beneath him. It swept him toward a central point, like the hole of a huge drain.

He ran faster.

The sand grew steeper.

He put his hands into play, paddling skyward as his feet flailed.

He continued slipping.

Soon he couldn't fight it any longer. He had to surrender. He gave it one last push—and found himself floating.

The heat was gone.

The light was gone.

The Earth was gone.

Suddenly he was drifting through darkness like the only person alive.

Gabriel appeared. "I can see that I've overwhelmed you," the archangel said, using Verrocchio's concerned voice. "You're sweating."

Leonardo wiped his brow and in that blink ended up back before the tablet, with the angel at his side. "Apparently you've given me more to think about than my mind can process in one sitting. In fact, I expect to be digesting your words for years to come."

"That's a good sign," Gabriel said. "A lack of struggle would indicate an inadequate mind. This is, after all, the greatest intellectual quest of all time."

"Nice play on words."

"Thank you."

"May I ask a question?"

"That's why I'm still here."

"What about prayer?"

Gabriel patted the short staff against his open palm. "Another intricate issue, but one worth addressing. According to some religions, God answers prayers. According to others, God does not. In any case, it's clear that the vast majority of prayers are not answered. If they were, nobody would be sick and everybody would be king."

"I can't argue with that."

"No, you can't. But as it happens, time does answer prayers, and more often than you think. Furthermore, when It does, It does so justly."

"How is that?" Leonardo asked.

"When we pray for something, we think about it. The more we pray, the more we think."

"Right...?"

"The more we think, the more we act. And the more we act, the more we solve. God does not answer prayers *for* us; God answers prayers *with* us."

Yet again, Leonardo found himself

surprised by the simplicity inherent in the archangel's fresh perspective.

Gabriel continued, "What could be more just than answering the prayers of those who work with God to achieve them. Those who devote time to their attainment? Are they not the most deserving?"

That sounded sensible. Leonardo would chew through it later, like a cow with its cud. For the moment, his mind was caught up in a new quandary. "I'm getting stuck on the notion of *spending time* when time is God."

"Yes, that's a prickly point. I'll cut straight to the conclusion, then lead you to it. Your mistake is confusing the tail, the traditional calendar view of time, with the whole elephant, time as God. That's no surprise. You've known the tail your whole life, but you've only just now caught a glimpse of the entire animal."

"So how do I bag the elephant?"

"Try tackling it with this observation. God gives people life, and what is life if not time?"

"What is life if not time?" As Leonardo repeated the words, another thought struck.

"Since God is time, God is constantly sharing itself with us."

"Correct."

"So what is death? Is death what happens when God abandons us?"

"Abandon is the wrong word. That viewpoint only considers that tail. The deceased are still in God's embrace. They still exist in time. They continue to send ripples forward and backward through God's universe. Think of it this way: *unallocated time is the thing the living have that the dead do not.*"

Unallocated time is the thing the living have that the dead do not. Leonardo's mind was bending so much he worried it would break. "So getting back to my original question. When I spend time on something, am I, in a sense, collaborating with God?"

"Well put. That is a crucial conclusion. The day's greatest takeaway. But don't let that revelation push you into the trap of extremism. The body God gave you has needs. The mind God gave you requires maintenance. Satisfying those is part of

God's system. Don't ignore them while trying to please God, for by doing so you will accomplish the opposite."

"So what should I be doing? To please God?"

"You know."

"I know?"

"God has given you a guide."

"It has? Why do I sense that this is another one of those things that's obvious once you know it?"

"Because you are wise beyond your years," Gabriel said, bringing his hands before his chest in a prayerful stance, before extending them forward as if giving a gift. "The guide God gave you is called *happiness*. You please God when you do today what will make you happy *tomorrow*. Happier *over time*."

"Happier over time," Leonardo repeated. "You mean doing things like eating sensibly and exercising both body and mind?"

"Exactly."

Gabriel waved a finger. "Now, let me caution you. Do not make the mistake of confusing *happiness* with *pleasure*. Pleasure feels like happiness in the moment, but beware. While there's nothing inherently wrong with pleasurable acts, their reward is fleeting. Without other balancing acts, they do not make you happier *over time*."

Leonardo pictured the faces he'd seen during his visits to the ghetto, jubilant when the wine was flowing but distraught the morning after. "So the wise person finds pleasures that pay dividends. Those that lead to happiness?"

"Perfectly put."

"You're giving me a lot to think about."

Gabriel flashed an impish look. "Don't worry. You have time."

"Good to know. May I push my luck? Ask another question?"

"By all means. The monks are still snoring and the sun is not rising."

"Thank you. Earlier, when I asked if dead things have been abandoned by God, you said the deceased still send ripples forward and backward through God's universe. What did you mean by that?"

"Ah, yes. Thank you for reminding me.

When an individual dies, time still exists. Other people still exist. As time moves forward, It carries the repercussions of what the deceased have done. In that way, the departed continue to impact the world, physically and mentally. They are praised and cursed every day, depending on and in proportion to the deeds they did while living."

The explanation sparked a further flash of insight. "That is the everlasting impact of one's life."

"Exactly. And that's the answer to your earlier question about how God could fairly judge *all* of an individual's actions. Each has an impact on God's kingdom. Each either enhances it or detracts from it—and the collective conscience knows which."

"And with that knowing, those actions travel forward in time."

"That's right. And—are you ready for this—they also travel backward."

"Backward?"

"Had your father been a mass murderer, for example, one might ask how a benevolent

God could permit him to live. The answer only comes a generation later—with you. In that sense, your actions travel backward—justifying your murderous father's existence."

"Fascinating. But that implies forethought. Are you suggesting that time knows where everything is going?"

"No. And you are right to call me out on that. My example was an oversimplification used to make a point. Time can't know where things are going. Not on the small scale. The individual scale. That's where personal choice comes into play. But time can predict where things are going on a grand scale because that's where averages apply.

"If you use the alphabet as the range of possible actions, some people will choose *A* and others *Z*, the extremes, but most will act in more moderate ways, around *M* or *N*. Furthermore, all must act in accordance with the laws of nature—and those are fixed in time."

The discussion was growing more esoteric by the minute, but Leonardo stuck with it.

He wanted to make the most of what might be his final meeting with Gabriel. "Do these ripples going forward and backward relate to Heaven and Hell? I feel there must be a connection."

"You're doing it again. Using Scripture as a guide, even though we've established that it is fundamentally flawed."

"Apologies. But somehow I sense that you have an answer for me anyway?"

Gabriel smiled. "We've already noted that our significant actions are praised or cursed by others, both contemporarily and in the future. But there's another aspect to punishment and reward that's much more personal."

"I'm all ears."

"Answer me this, Leonardo. As you look back on life and consider the choices you made, is there anything worse than opportunity lost? Anything more gratifying than time well spent?"

"Nothing leaps to mind."

Gabriel crossed his arms. "Hell is wasting your time. Heaven is spending your time wisely."

"Brilliant," Leonardo whispered.

"Most people don't consciously make the connection, of course. But everyone experiences the impact."

Overwhelmed and temporarily out of questions, Leonardo found himself frowning. The longer it lasted, the more his elevated mood became eclipsed by a sense of sorrow.

He knew the reason. "Are we done?"

"There is one more thing I'm pleased to point out," Gabriel said as his image faded. "You'll be able to finish *The Last Supper* now—without worry."

The Archangel was right, Leonardo realized. Time had no face. To be accurate and appropriate, the Son of God had only to be a human reflection of Its benevolent force.

As Gabriel vanished, Leonardo awoke.

Energized by the power of his newfound wisdom and encouraged by his fresh understanding, Leonardo reached for his brush. He had one last portrait to paint.

Politics

Leonardo found Niccolò Machiavelli waiting for him when he dismounted the scaffolding for the final time. "Finished at last?"

"Finished at last," Leonardo confirmed with a happy heart. "What brings you here?"

"I got word that you put Prior Gioffre's face on Judas. Actually, I think all of Milan now knows. It's a hot topic of conversation."

"Yes, I've been summoned to see Duke Sforza."

"And yet you're here?"

"Sforza doesn't give a whit about Prior Gioffre. I'm sure he was chuckling on the inside while his lips humored the malevolent monk."

"But still, Sforza won't want to run afoul of the church."

"I've got that covered. All I have to do is point out that Gioffre is committing the sin of pride by comparing himself to one of Jesus's disciples. Then I'll announce that *The Last Supper* is complete. Sforza will declare victory and close the case, happy to have delivered on his promise."

"And the king will soon marvel at your mural. Outstanding! Your political reflexes are improving, my friend."

"I'm learning from the best. Why are you really here, Niccolò?"

Speaking with unusual verve, Niccolò said, "Cesare Borgia wants to see me."

Leonardo didn't immediately grasp the cause for his friend's excitement. "I don't see you joining the church, Niccolò."

"You haven't heard? Cesare isn't a

cardinal anymore. He resigned. He's the first cardinal in history to do so."

"But he's the son of the Pope."

"And now he's also Duke of Valentinois. Louis XII bestowed the title on him the same day he hung up his red robe. Now Cesare has a major principality to run—and he will certainly need help doing it. Papal support only goes so far."

"That explains your enthusiasm."

"Indeed. It would be unwise for me to keep him waiting, so I must return to Florence at once. But I didn't want to leave Milan without sharing in your celestial secret. I trust you were blessed by another appearance?"

"Yes. The final visit." Now Leonardo's voice was the one with verve.

"Sounds like the story has a satisfactory ending?"

"Entirely satisfactory. Ride with me to Sforza Castle and I'll tell you all about it."

While walking toward the refectory door, Leonardo ordered that the scaffolding be dismantled at once. A tactical move designed to discourage any attempt at comebacks.

Once he and Niccolò had trotted off the church grounds and away from eager ears, Leonardo recounted Gabriel's final visits. Da Vinci concluded with the same open-ended question he'd used to start their first discussion back at the Blackbird. "What do you think?"

"I'm embarrassed that I didn't make the link myself. Unlike you, I've always looked at religious doctrine with a skeptical eye. But I never made that simple connection."

"So you concur that time and God are one and the same?"

"Gabriel left no logical room for doubt. There's nothing else that comes close, and substituting the...what did you call it? The *wizened old man with a wand* now seems all the more preposterous."

Leonardo was grateful for the sanity check. Especially one so unambiguous and enthusiastic. Despite the disciplined discussion and celestial confirmation, subconsciously he had harbored a hint of doubt.

Since Niccolò was short on time, Leonardo proceeded directly to the big question. "You're the master strategist. Tell me, what's the best way to spread the word?"

Niccolò stopped his mount so abruptly that its hooves dislodged stones.

Leonardo turned Euclid about and drew close.

"Don't even think about sharing what you've learned."

Niccolò's hissed words struck Leonardo like a slap to the face. "But I must. This knowledge will end the religious strife that has rocked the planet for centuries. It will help people to better direct their lives. It will comfort and console them."

Niccolò shook his head as though addressing an adolescent child. "It will never happen. You'll just become the latest victim."

"Latest victim? What are you talking about?

"Remember Savonarola?"

"The Dominican friar behind the bonfire of the vanities?"

"That's right. Alexander VI didn't like the

power Savonarola was amassing with his brand of religion, so the church charged him with heresy and burned him at the stake. You might not get the torch if you don't directly criticize the Pope, but under the very best of circumstances, you'll still spend the rest of your life defending your blasphemy from the confines of a cold cave."

"But it's in humanity's best interest to know."

"True. Nonetheless, everyone will resist it. The revelation would threaten many of society's core beliefs and shake Italy's entire power structure."

"But it's the truth!"

Niccolò scoffed. "The truth is what the people in power tell you it is."

Leonardo didn't know how to respond. Niccolò was right, but at the same time he had to be wrong.

While Leonardo flailed, Niccolò pressed his point. "Few will be smart enough to follow the logic. Perhaps if people were starting with a blank slate, but of course they're not. Those intelligent enough to understand and accept your argument will be either too shrewd or too scared to admit it."

"But why?"

"Fear of retribution, Leonardo. Plain and simple. The Pope is the most powerful person on the planet. His Holiness owes his position to the religious status quo. And I assure you, Alexander VI is nothing if not ruthless."

"You're too cynical. Surely others will add their voice to mine. If not in Italy, then abroad."

"Who? Nobody can make money off the news. Nobody can rally people behind a God that neither asks anything from them nor promises special favors. For the same reason, nobody can gain personal power from this revelation.

"On the other hand, every organization already in the God business will lose if this news becomes widely accepted. They will fight it with everything they have. They will fight *you* with everything they have. You'll become too controversial to employ as an artist or engineer. No church or government will touch you. Bear in mind, kings count on the church to help them cling to power."

Leonardo's heart sank to a new low. "Now that you mention it, I must admit that your warning rings true."

Still, Leonardo had his doubts. He hated to be so cynical.

"I can see you waffling," Niccolò said. "Don't. It's worse than we discussed."

"Worse? How can it be worse?"

"People often don't want the truth. They can't handle it. In this instance that is doubly so."

"Why?"

Niccolò took a moment to compose his reply. "While designing all your weapons of war, you spent time with soldiers, right? You studied battles and tactics? You heard the horror stories? Saw the carnage?"

"Yes, I did."

"Then answer me this: Did you meet a single soldier who did not want to believe that the wizened old man was on his side when the swords started swinging? Men desperately want to hope that He will intervene on their behalf. Guide their arrows. Govern their attacks. You cannot overcome that primal desire with logic."

"Not everyone is a soldier. And there will be far fewer soldiers if this knowledge eliminates religious wars."

"It's not just soldiers who do battle, Leonardo. Life isn't easy, and most people battle for the majority of theirs. They want to think they're not in the fight alone. They want to believe there's an omnipotent hand available to help them."

"But nobody ever actually gets the help of that hand. He doesn't reach down from Heaven and swat their problems away."

"It doesn't matter. They get something else. They get hope. Right there, right then, they get a mental reprieve. Hope may not be as omnipotent as time, but it is a powerful force."

"You're right," Leonardo admitted. As he spoke, a shocking insight struck. *Perhaps he wasn't the first to know.* "Is that why nobody has ever announced God's true identity before? It's not that nobody has ever figured it out, it's that anybody clever enough to do so was also wise enough to realize that spreading the word would be suicide?"

Niccolò brought hand to chin. "I hadn't thought about it, but now that you mention it, I'm sure that's an accurate appraisal."

"So after all the excitement, the end result is—nothing?"

Again Niccolò assumed the posture of a parent. "Far from it, my friend. You now know what worship really means. To honor God is to make the most of your life. To make every minute count. That's incredibly motivating. I think it will make you more productive than ever."

Leonardo considered that aspect of his windfall. "Gabriel said something similar. Still, it's going to be weird, going through life, knowing history's greatest secret—and keeping it to myself."

They descended into silence, both men processing pictures of what it was going to be like living with that incredible insight— while keeping quiet about it. An astounding secret all their own.

After a couple of contemplative minutes, Leonardo caught Niccolò staring at him with an intrigued expression.

"What is it?" Leonardo asked.

"Your face. It's got the most unusual smile."

Mona Lisa

Leonardo Da Vinci. 1500s

Afterword

Dear Reader,

I hope you enjoyed Leonardo and Gabriel, and consider the read to be time well spent. I also hope your mind continues spinning long after the pages have stopped flipping.

Leonardo and Gabriel is a little book of big questions and auspicious answers. Odds are, you're still processing a few. I have a couple of recommendations to help aid your digestion. But first, let me note that my goal as the author is to stimulate thought, not proselytize. I'm attempting to answer questions that have been confronting and confounding humanity for thousands of years in the hope that the process will help readers of all creeds to live more fulfilling lives.

My first recommendation is that you reread the novella, including the introduction, paying particular attention to everything Gabriel says. The second is to remember the archangel's *Blank Slate* and *Elephant* lessons.

Bear in mind as you reread that *borrowed learning* is what leads people astray. If you find yourself pulling external references into your internal debate, try to focus on the inherent logic instead.

While considering the conclusion, apply the elephant analogy to your own understanding of time. Before this book, you knew the tail. Now that you've listened to Leonardo and Gabriel debate, you likely see time as much more than mere ticks on a clock.

Regarding the last point, it's worth bringing Einstein into the discussion— something Leonardo and Gabriel couldn't do in fifteenth century Italy. I'm not going to get into relativity here as it's both too complex a theory to fit this format, and too incomplete to be much more than a distraction. Rather, I'll invite those of you inclined to interject astrophysics, to step into Leonardo's shoes and answer a few questions for yourself:

Which came first, time or space?

Can either exist without the other?

Given their absolute interdependence, is it not sensible to consider time and space like the tail and tusks of the same entity, namely Time with a capital T.

About the Author

Given the nature of this book, it's appropriate to share a bit about my background. Both my grandfathers were ministers. Whereas one died young, the other helped raise me. He was a prominent figure in the Presbyterian church, and I a favorite grandchild. My father, who is now retired from Boston University, was a philosophy and education professor. My mother, an accomplished tax consultant. I graduated Hanover College in 1990 as a philosophy and math major and later earned master's degrees in business administration and international studies from the University of Pennsylvania.

Before becoming an author, I enjoyed three successful careers: a military career in my early twenties, working in Soviet Counterintelligence with the US Army Special Forces, the Green Berets; a corporate career from mid-twenties to early-thirties, running international operations for blue-chip medical companies, based out of Moscow and Brussels; and a medical startup career from late-thirties to late-forties, as a Silicon Valley senior executive and CEO.

Leonardo and Gabriel is my tenth book. As an author, it is a departure for me. Whereas this novella is essentially a philosophy text disguised as a thriller, my other books are pure thrillers—with strong philosophical foundations. Not coincidentally, my latest is titled *The Price of Time*. Imagine a mashup of Michael Crichton and Agatha Christie written in the same style as *Leonardo and Gabriel*.

Google "Tigner" or go to amazon.com/author/tigner to learn more.

Made in the USA
Coppell, TX
11 January 2021